ARCHILOCHOS

The endpapers show the funerary stone of Glaukos, son of Leptines (Archilochos' friend addressed on pp. 8 and 32). It is still on Thasos. The inscription states that the stone was erected by the sons of Brentes, about whom nothing is now known. It is carved in the Parian script (which had an alphabet of only twenty-two letters), boustrophedonic – literally, "as the ox turns" – the first line being from left to right, the second from right to left and in "mirror writing", and the third from left to right again.

The Greek text used is M. L. West's *Iambi et Elegi Graeci*, with the exception of the Cologne epode which is taken from D. L. Page's *Supplementum Lyricum Graecum*. The numbering of the fragments otherwise follows West's, except for the fragment on p. 34 which he attributes to Hipponax.

ARCHILOCHOS

Introduced, translated and illustrated by

MICHAEL AYRTON

with an essay by
G. S. Kirk

Secker & Warburg
London

First published in England 1977 by
Martin Secker & Warburg Limited
14 Carlisle Street, London W1V 6NN

SBN 436 02853 0

Printed in Great Britain by
Westerham Press Limited,
Westerham, Kent
Bound by
W. & J. Mackay Limited,
Chatham, Kent

CONTENTS

LIST OF PLATES

INTRODUCTION

Michael Ayrton

I seemed to see in my mind a hard and heavy man, raising himself after a restless sleep and lifting his head from his crossed arms as if his elbows were tired. Yet from where I sat opposite to him, across the table, he could reach my right hand and this he did, locking it in his own and casually bending my wrist and elbow back against their joints. Such a table contest is not new among drinkers who are neither friendly nor at particular odds.

Without effort, he bent my arm back and down on to the table so that my wine cup broke into shards. I was not surprised that he put me down so easily. He was two and a half thousand years younger than I and his living depended on his arms; his right arm armed with the spear, his left with the expendable shield, or more memorably with the lyre.

I would not say that this seasoned man smiled, but rather that he grinned sardonically. What he said, I did not understand, but it was laconic. What passed between us was not speech, but in the act of putting my arm down against my will and by breaking the cup with my strained knuckles, I found him established, out of time, in the first person singular. And that in my time he is; the first in the first person, self established peremptorily. His chosen name "Archilochos" means First Sergeant. Perhaps he stood first in that rank too, neither envying his officers nor sparing them his mockery.

What was I to do with these shards of a broken cup, those venomous *ostraka*, those splinters of loved landscape and lost love in the spilled black rage, staining the unscrubbed table which drinks the wine down into its grain? I am drunk with Archilochos, from his Ismarian vintage, strained unmixed from a *krater*, which by its approximate date erases the temptation to see him dressed in pastiche of Exekias, not yet born. Nor is this mercenary, whose gifts came equally from the war god, Enyalios, and from the Muses and who also knew the metres of Dionysos and of Demeter, any *kouros* of his time with rudimentary thorax, stiff arms and unwavering smile, but a man pared down to the meshed moving parts of a man and as tough as a goat.

What do I know of him whose, to me, incomprehensible tongue is known, even to scholars, only from later quotation and from the tatters of papyrus copies of copies, found wrapped, for want of other packing, around Alexandrian mummies? What have I learned? That he was a Parian? Paros I know and neither the island's armature nor its fig trees can be so changed since he was there. That he went to Thasos and perhaps thereafter fought in Thrace? Being a wandering man, he knew and spoke of the valley of the river Siris which flows in the instep of Italy. The Siris I have seen and also Thasos. From mainland Thrace, its contours are still seen to be bristling with pine trees, still like the backbone of an ass. The Siris remains a river in fertile land, although it has shifted in its bed. I doubt if the natural light changes over these places in one millennium more than another, or that last year's solar eclipse would have differed to the eye from the one that Archilochos surely must have seen to have recorded it so personally. He was the first poet to speak personally of an eclipse. To him it came as an event which left nothing ever to be surprised by again, but he surprised me, by his grip on me, twenty-five centuries after the Naxians killed him. It was a man called Kallondes, nicknamed "Crow", who killed Archilochos, by fair means or foul. And at Delphi, the Pythia turned Kallondes out of the temple, for the murder of one who had been beloved of Apollo and a servant of the Muses. She sent the Crow to Tainaron, to expiate the blood guilt.

Archilochos was not a man readily to be appeased and one given, it seems, to more ferocity than twisting the arm of an unborn stranger. As to the latter act, it was casual, unpremeditated, doubtless an idle movement of his wrist, but it has thrust images upon me to my alarm, since it was said of him, eight hundred years after his death, that his tomb should be avoided since it remained a nest of hornets. To find that tomb, one should watch for hornets. No trace of it is known.

It is said of Archilochos that he was frustrated in his deepest love of Neoboulé the daughter of Lykambes whom he came to hate. It is said of Archilochos that he was a bastard – a right bastard. It is said of him that he destroyed Lykambes with his verses and that the daughters of Lykambes hanged themselves from shame. It is said that Archilochos was not scrupulous in honour, being aware of himself as no participant in Homeric epic; being instead enduring and professional in both his vocations and given to making use of the dying oral tradition as it suited him. Else would he have confessed to having thrown away his shield and run shrewdly from the odds? He was no conventional hero and he makes few boasts.

So what do I know that I must celebrate but his presence and the endurance of rocks, of the flexing sea, of women, of friends, of animals and bitter enemies. The poems he left, now shattered, were once handled by great poets and learned grammarians who knew all his works and acknowledged his uncanny skill with metres, even while they reviled his attacking spirit and remarked for centuries his relentless ferocity. Even they would not have known the music of his sung lyrics even if, enviably, they and their descendants could seem to hear his speaking voice as I cannot. What I have of Archilochos rests only in part on an idea of the appearance of his verses blocked in Parian capitals, when even the Greek alphabet was as new to men as the typewriter is to us. And these are in the mind's eye. No line of his verse survives from his own hand, nor even in his alphabet.

All I know rests on his landscape, on the sound of hornets in fig trees and the sight in my mind of how he looked and how the light cut through the holes in the curtain hung over an unglazed window, in the place where he twisted my arm. As to that gesture, it felt more physical than metaphysical since it was his strong grip on his known world and the long lasting thongs of his sinews, hardened by thrusts, that I feel still in my arm and shoulder as if no time separated him from me.

I do not know much Greek and so Geoffrey Kirk made me a literal translation of the existing texts, all that can be comprehensibly transcribed of them. I took this and I acknowledge also a debt to Richard Lattimore, Guy Davenport, F. Lasserre, D. A. Campbell and others, whose translations and discourses I have read. But I rashly composed this text myself.

I have made sixteen etchings and used them to link various quite separate fragments to which the images seem to me relevant. Some are arranged ambiguously and with a deliberate irony which is my own. Their juxtaposition may be quite fortuitous, but ambiguity is present in the verse, I believe, in many fragments, not entirely because they are fragments. Some images sequentially follow that of Neoboulé, whose hand Archilochos wished he could touch, in a line from a poem which may have been the first love lyric written in Europe. Lykambes, her father, follows her and then the creatures of the beast fables, now known to us from Aesop, but which appear to be linked, by Archilochos, to his satires on Lykambes. As for Neoboulé, her younger sister replaced her in a fashion that Archilochos delicately described; this in a long, relatively newly discovered fragment of an epode, perhaps written early enough for his beard not to have been "darkened" at the time. But since no chronology of the poems is known, this may reflect Archilochos' youth in retrospect. That his beard did darken, I am in no doubt. I show Archilochos naked, because he is, to me, the most naked man who ever wrote.

My etchings do not illustrate the fragments literally. They are set beside them in some spirit of piety and were made to get the cramps out of my hand and arm for which he was responsible. I must risk the hornets.

THE FRAGMENTS

2 My barley bread is kneaded in my spear
And in my spear flows my Ismarian wine
Leaning upon my spear, I drink.

1 I serve the lord Enyalios, but I know
the Muses' lovely gift.

19 I am not jealous of Gyges, nor his gold
nor envy the gods their power, nor lust for kingdoms.
I do not spare a glance beyond my craft.

216 They'll say I really was a Carian mercenary . . .

128 Heart in confusion, faltering start to beat.
Rise and ward off the spears of foes and fight.
Winning, disdain display. Defeat's no reason to collapse and moan.
If you are grieved, then grieve. In joy, rejoice,
indulging in excess of neither one.
What must be done is recognise a rhythm.

324 Tenella Kallinike.
Hail, Lord Herakles triumphant
Tenella Kallinike.
Yourself and Iolaos, warriors both
Tenella Kallinike.

114 I don't like a long-legged, straddling captain,
a cockscomb curled, but part chin-shaven.
Let him be short and thickset, solid,
firm on his feet, bowlegged, full of heart.

15 Glaukos, a mercenary is a friend for just so long as he's fighting.

131/2 The dispositions of men, Glaukos, son of Leptines,
are from day to day as Zeus makes them,
and their thoughts are governed by circumstance, nothing else.

331 A wild fig tree growing among rocks, feeder of many crows,
easy, accessible, loved by all, a cheap feast for strangers.

42 . . . as through a tube a Thracian or a Phrygian sucks down barley-beer,
and she was leaning forward, working . . .

184 In one hand she carried water, in her guile,
in the other, fire . . .

116 Farewell to Paros and those figs and the life of the sea . . .

166, 3 Paros, the lovely . . .

Cologne Papyrus 3511

. . . simply restrain yourself . . .
Or if you can't, if you're set on it, wild for it
think nearer home. There, in our house, is a girl
who is blameless. She is a virgin. I think she's lovely,
tender and gentle. She you neglect and she yearns to be married.
Why then grieve her?
This was her plea so I formally answered:
"Daughter of her whom we mourn, Amphimedo,
excellent lady, laid now in dark earth,
there are sweet gifts for young men from the goddess,
pleasures that stop at the brink of fulfilment.
One will suffice.
If the god wills, we'll consider the other.
When my beard darkens, let us discuss it.
But for the moment, whatever it costs me, I will obey:
pour my libation out at your gateway, out in the grass.
Do not deny me the threshold, beloved
I'll not break in.
As for Neoboulé, she is for others.
Let who will have her, such as will take her.
She is full blown and her grace is gone from her.
Knowing no bounds to her love of excess.
Let no one wish such a woman on me.
She's for the crows.
I won't be mocked by the neighbours, or laughed at.
She'd spring a child on me, in her ambition,
blind and untimely, drop me an offspring.
She's like the bitch in the proverb, she's feckless,
having excess in her nature, she's mad.
I prefer you."
This said, I laid the girl down among flowers;
in my soft cloak I enwrapped and embraced her
gently I touched all her flesh with my hands.
She like a fawn remained still but she trembled
as she revealed her fresh down I flowed onto it;
shot my white strength.

3 Expect no slingshots, nor will bows be stretched
when Ares builds this battle on the plain.
There will be pain-filled work, close in, for swords
for that is what those men are expert at,
Lords of Euboea, famous for their spears . . .

101 We, a thousand, are the slaughterers of the seven who fell.
We overtook them with our running feet . . .

108 Hear, Lord Hephaistos, here I clasp your knees.
Favour me. Fight by my side.
Grant me what is yours to grant . . .

94 Athena, daughter of Zeus the thunderer, stood at their side in battle,
stirring the woeful army, gave them heart. But as she drove that day,
over the earth, her song sounded a wholly different tune,
so that the fields lay thick with those released
. . . but by the will of the Olympian gods . . .

12 Let us hide the painful gifts of the Lord Poseidon . . .

8 On the open sea, grey, salt, high curled as hair,
we pray often, all of us, pray for a safe return . . .

192 Of fifty men, Poseidon, lord of horses, left only Koiranos.

213 . . . having their souls in the embrace of waves . . .

134 For it is not noble to sneer at those who died.

13 How can we feast in the city, Perikles, when we must mourn
With proper grief those lost in the pounding sea?
They are submerged; we grieve with swollen lungs,
but the gods, my friend, give us the strength to hold,
to endure the bloody wound and cease to weep.
Such a turn will come to others another time,
but since our time is now, let us face the facts;
tears are for women; put them aside and quick.

122 Now nothing can surprise us any more; nothing be unexpected,
now that Zeus, Olympian father, bringing night at noon,
has put the shining sun out, put pale fear in men.
From that time, everything became possible, everything.
Dolphins might now exchange with animals and leap into the hills. Don't doubt.
Beasts could desert the forest for the sea. They could prefer
as pasture ocean's echoing waves to woods, water to fields.
Let no one marvel if that comes about, nor swear it couldn't happen . . .

30/31 She rejoiced in myrtle and the fair flower of the rose
and her hair poured shadow down her shoulders and her back.

118 Neoboulé, would I could touch her hand . . .

119 . . . and fall, a labourer to his flask, attach
belly to belly, flank to flank.

191 . . . for such a passion of lust coiled under my heart,
and poured a dense mist over my eyes,
stealing the fragile senses out of my breast . . .

193 In desolation I lie fainting with desire,
wracked by the will of the gods,
harsh pains piercing my bones.

38 Such was the elder daughter of Lykambes . . .

172 What sort of contrivance is this, father Lykambes?
Who has got at you? What became of the wits
you once had? Among the citizens, you have become
a laugh . . .

173 You have forgotten a great oath,
salt and table . . .

188 No bloom left by now and old age coming on.
Hideous with your skin dried out in furrows . . .

205 You, an old woman, would not scent yourself
if you weren't out of your mind . . .

201 The fox knows many tricks, the hedgehog only one; a good one.

174 This is a fable of men
of a compact made between fox and eagle . . .

177 O Zeus, father Zeus, yours is the power of heaven
and you watch over the works of men,
the evil and the upright. And the beasts,
the vain and noble, these are your concern . . .

168 Charilaos, son of Erasmon
I will tell you a comic story which
you will consider, old friend,
to be a great joke . . .

185 I will tell you a story, son of Keryx,
one with a dreadful outcome.
A monkey went alone into the border lands,
cut off from other creatures, isolated.
A vixen met him.
She had a subtle cunning . . .

187 . . . having such a bottom, oh monkey . . .

176 You see on that high rock,
rugged and sheer,
he sits, jeering at your prowess . . .

41 . . . a sea crow, rocking on a jutting cliff,
shaking her wings and working at her trade . . .

23 Woman, don't worry, don't fear gossip.
Sometime tonight I shall deal with the matter,
so let me have your heart . . .

I know how to love who loves me
and to return hate with hate. Don't you know who I am,
or my lineage, that you should rate me so low?
Do I seem so reduced?

No men have ever sacked this city you now hold.
Rule her, rejoice in being tyrant,
you who have won great fame at spearpoint.
When even ants get angry, Myrmex,
theirs is the triumph and the glory.
You will be envied by the many . . .

93a . . . Peisistratos' son
led men to Thasos, skilled with flute and lyre,
bringing pure gold with them for Thracian dogs.
They made a common ill for their own gain . . .

120 I know the dithyramb for the lord Dionysos
I chant it drunk, and thunderstruck with wine . . .

124b . . . you drank too much, you drank your wine unmixed
and did not offer any contribution
nor did you come as a friend does when we asked you,
but took in such a skinful that you sank your wits.
Your belly led you into shamelessness . . .

4 You need your wine cup; go across the swift ship's benches
unseal the stuff and strain it off the lees.
Do it; we won't be sober on this watch.

43 . . . his prick, full as a corn-stuffed jackass,
a Prienian jackass . . . overflowed.

35 We have a working ox at home, with lofty horns.
He knows his work, knows how to plough a furrow.

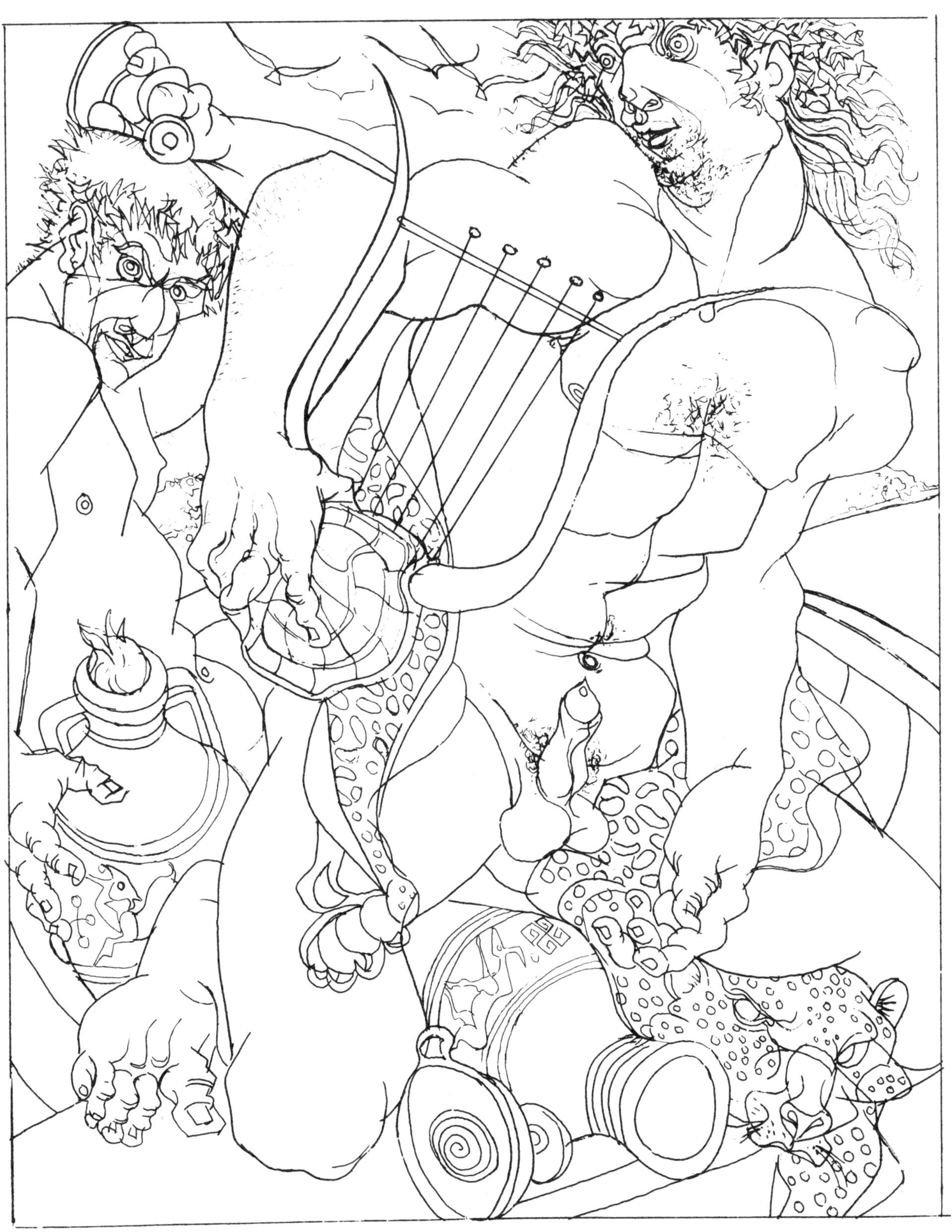

105 Glaukos, look: the uneasy sea is stirred.
Cloud-sign of storm stands on the Gyrean height,
the unexpected grips us, breeding fear . . .

21/22 Here this island stands, pine crested, bristling like a donkey's back.
This is no fine nor lovely place,
nor desirable as are the streams of Siris . . .

102 All the griefs of all the Hellenes came together in Thasos . . .

212 It stood on the edge of wind, on the edge of wave . . .

228 Thasos, thrice-grievous city . . .

[Hipponax] . . . stranded ashore from the sea.
115 And in Salmydessos, may the screw-haired men,
the Thracians, receive their guest most kindly, naked.
There let him taste all bitterness fulfilled,
chew evil, bite the bread of slavery.
Doglike, face downwards, may he lie in scum
and after, mess of seaweed cover him.
May his teeth rattle. Rigid from the cold
let him sprawl, helpless, on the scouring shore.
This I would like to see become of him,
this man who broke his given word to me,
this man who wronged me, trod upon his oath,
my erstwhile comrade.

126 . . . but I know one thing and a great one;
how to repay with evil him who injures me.

5 One of the Saites struts with my shield since I, unwillingly,
left it under a bush, but I got away fast.
So what do I care about that piece of armour, good as it was?
To hell with the thing. I can get another, no worse.

133 No man is respected among us, once he is dead.
We the living look to the man alive.
It is the dead who always get the worst.

14 Aisimedes, no one who heeds the noise of critics
would experience much in the way of satisfaction.

127 I made a mistake – a misfortune which has, I suppose, come upon other men . . .

ESSAY

G. S. Kirk

Archilochos was one of the most remarkable, as well as one of the most idiosyncratic, of the Greek poets. He was recognised by the Greeks themselves as one of the main founders of the tradition of personal poetry with which the non-choral lyric became identified, and which reached its peak with Sappho; and, as a result, considerable fragments of his work survive. He stands, chronologically as in other respects, between the epic and the classical worlds, between Homer and Hesiod on the one hand and Pindar and the great dramatists on the other. Homer composed his great epics probably around 700 B.C., and Hesiod came soon after. Archilochos comes soon after that, for he can be placed with reasonable security near the middle of the seventh century B.C. Herodotus described him as contemporary with Gyges of Lydia (to whom the poet referred), and Gyges reigned from about 687 to about 651. The poet also mentioned a disaster suffered by the Magnesians, and that is likely to have been the destruction of their city by the Treres in 652. Lastly the eclipse of the sun alluded to in frag. 122 (p. 18) is evidently a recent event, surely that of 648 B.C. rather than its predecessor of 711.

Archilochos belongs, then, to an era in which the oral tradition that culminated in the *Iliad* and *Odyssey* was fading, or had virtually expired. He himself must have known the works of Homer and his immediate successors extremely well. His verses are full of epic phraseology, sometimes cleverly adapted to fresh metres that are iambic rather than dactylic in impulse. But the subject-matter of his poetry is entirely new. The mythological past is almost totally abandoned; only the gods intrude from time to time – Ares or Enyalios, the god of war, Poseidon who rules over the sea, Zeus who punishes injustice among animals, now, as well as among men. The heroic world of Thebes and Troy, the great legendary figures of Perseus, Jason, Theseus and Herakles, are virtually absent from his poetry, and that is remarkable in itself. In their place Archilochos sets his own Aegean ambience, his own experiences and passions and rules for living. His native land is Paros, one of the two big islands at the heart of the Cyclades. His father Telesikles had led the expedition that won Thasos, in the northern Aegean off the coast of Thrace, as a Parian colony. Archilochos himself voyaged to Thasos and fought from it, just as he also fought against Paros' neighbour and rival, Naxos; indeed ancient tradition declared that he was killed by a Naxian. Life at that particular period was not short of challenges and vicissitudes, and Archilochos was clearly not a man to be deterred by either.

His complexities and contradictions give him an additional fascination, even among the poets of the archaic age. Admittedly Alkman is now known to have written cosmogonical poetry as well as his delightful and enigmatic Maiden Song, but Kallinos and Tyrtaios kept fairly strictly within the bounds of martial and patriotic elegy, and Stesichoros' choral versions of traditional myths begin to look a little stereotyped as more fragments become known. At the turn of the seventh and sixth centuries Alkaios rivals Archilochos in partisan fire but lacks his versatility and imagination, and it is only Sappho that surpasses him both technically and in spiritual brilliance. Archilochos had not, of course, achieved as she did the true melic stanza, although his epodes moved towards it. He was, none the less, a metrical virtuoso, equally adept at elegiacs, at trochaic tetrameters, at iambic trimeters and at various epodic combinations.

This range is balanced by a startling variety of tone and subject, extending from the moralistic and reflective through the passionate and purely lyrical to the sardonic and the scabrous. Many of even the more innocuous-looking fragments are thought by his latest and best editor to have been obscene in their implication, and West may be right. Archilochos was notorious in antiquity for his poetical attacks on Lykambes, a Parian aristocrat, and his daughters, one of whom, Neoboulé, had been promised him in marriage and then insultingly withheld. He turned his full armoury of verses (not only the iambics that became the classic vehicle for obloquy) against this unfortunate family, and the story was that they hanged themselves in despair. Untrue, perhaps; but we have only to read some of the surviving fragments about women engaged in spectacular sexual action – 41 or 42 (pp. 26, 10), for instance, not to speak of the new Cologne fragment (p. 12) – to see how degraded the poet's victims might feel. How much of all this was the genuine rage and grief of Archilochos himself, and how much the exploitation of an abuse-theme that could conceivably have been traditional, we cannot precisely tell. Those fragmentary pieces read very personally; but so, to a lesser degree, does the deprecation of a tyrant's life (frag. 19, p. 6) that as Aristotle tells us was not spoken by the poet in his own person. It might still have reproduced his views, but there is a dramatic element in his work, exemplified in his use of animal-fables as one means of deriding Lykambes, that warns us against taking every isolated statement as a direct indication of his own feelings.

It is a debated question how far Archilochos reacted against the Homeric tradition and its values. No one living at his time and sensitive to literature could be indifferent to a tradition that continued to influence Hellenic life and thought down to its declining days; but to assign Archilochos to one side or another, Homeric or anti-Homeric, is too simple-minded. Even "Homer" is an amalgam of distinct and sometimes contradictory ideas and standards, and the monumental epics are a blend of the relics of late-Mycenaean chivalry and feudalism with the misunderstandings, exaggerations and humanisations of many generations of later transmitters.

When Archilochos opts for a stocky, bandy-legged general rather than a coxcomb, as he does in frag. 114 (p. 8), he is clearly elaborating a line of thought suggested by the deceptively unimpressive figure of Odysseus as described by Helen in the third book of the *Iliad*. That may be Homer's own amendment of the heroic archetype. But even the unamended tradition asks us to admire no coxcombs, and Archilochos is reacting here not against Homeric ideals but against more contemporary attitudes and personalities. This same Odysseus would surely not have hesitated to abandon his shield if necessary (as Hugh Lloyd-Jones has observed), just as our poet did according to frag. 5 (p. 36); although he would not have been so wonderfully cynical about it – or is "stoical" the better term? At any rate Archilochos is far from simple in this sort of poem, neither wholly Homeric (in any of the senses of the word) nor wholly the reverse, but developing new attitudes that are already adumbrated here and there in the *Iliad* or *Odyssey*, and transforming heroic resignation and self-pity into an embryonic philosophy of passionate and sardonic self-control. Despite his frequent shafts of heroic reference, in language rather than in subject, Archilochos turns out in the end to be a novel sort of creature: individualistic to the point of eccentricity, self-reliant, not too different in certain ways from the mercenary soldier to whom he apparently compared himself in frag. 216 (p. 6) – yet in other respects obviously quite distinct, not only in his poetical skill and imagination but also because of the loyalty to friends and city that shines out from his verses and is characteristic of the evolving civic ethos of the archaic age.

The split between the old heroic world as enshrined and enlarged in Homer and the new world of colonialism and exploration, of the growing-pains of political self-awareness, of the emergence of the individual, is one of the more intriguing aspects of Archilochos and his poetry; and we cannot hope to judge the poetry properly unless we begin to understand the split. He admires the Euboean aristocrats for their old-fashioned tradition of close fighting (frag. 3, p. 14), but believes in assuaging the discomfort of a watch at sea by opening the wine-casks and getting drunk (frag. 4, p. 30). His sorrow for comrades killed or drowned is passionately felt, and he sees the cruelty and futility of much that happens in war, but rallies his heart with a call to control emotion and adjust itself to circumstances (frag. 128, p. 6) that is significantly different from Odysseus' "endure, heart, for you have suffered worse before" in Homer. Achilles whiles away his time in the ninth book of the *Iliad* by singing heroic ditties, but Archilochos' profession in frag. 1 (p. 6) of being a servant both of the lord Enyalios and of the Muses implies a totally different view of the place of fighting and poetry in the world – especially when one adds that for him being a poet also involves singing dithyrambs when "thunderstruck with wine", for the essentially unheroic Dionysos (frag. 120, p. 30).

It is a cruel accident that we have so little of Archilochos' martial poetry. He was respected rather than much read in later antiquity, but even so a good deal of it *almost* survives, both in the occasional papyrus fragment from Graeco-Roman Egypt and in two inscriptions erected in his memory in his native island in the third and first centuries B.C.; but in each case either the beginnings or the ends of the verses are missing. These poems, mainly in trochaic tetrameters, obviously told of the colonising and consolidating of Thasos, of campaigns against and negotiations with the Thracians of the facing coast, of skirmishes between Paros itself and its neighbour Naxos across the narrow strait that separated them. Yet somehow their essence and real drift fail to come through the gaps on papyrus or stone, even despite a multitude of intelligible phrases, and we cannot tell what the poet's attitude was or why he wrote on this kind of topic at such length. I do not myself conclude that he was so one-sidedly a fighting man as Alkaios, for example, was political zealot. The other sides of life, including love-making, revenge, philosophising, poetry itself, occupied him as well. But in any event a man's poetry is not always an accurate index of his lifetime concerns, and convention as well as momentary passion plays its part. Archilochos was, more than most, a creature of the moment. "Farewell to Paros and those figs and the life of the sea," he wrote in frag. 116 (p. 10); but surely that is an emotional exaggeration – for could he ever escape from the sea, in Thasos itself or by travelling to southern Italy and seeing the river Siris as frag. 22 (p. 32) implies?

The poet's longest and most complete fragment came to light only recently when a papyrus sheet that had been used to form part of an Egyptian mummy-case was unfolded by a new process. It is Cologne papyrus 3511 and is translated by Michael Ayrton on p. 12. Presumably part of the complex diatribe against Lykambes and his daughters, it shows much of Archilochos' diversity, his cynicism towards women as well as his occasional tenderness as a purely erotic poet. He contrives to discredit the elder sister, presumably Neoboulé although her name is not mentioned, by asserting that an overactive love-life has made her old as well as disreputable. At the same time he is intent on calming the fears of the younger girl, to whom he depicts himself as talking, by suggesting that they can take their pleasure together in other ways if she is scared to make love completely. His persuasion is successful, and he lays her in the grass and has his way; but did he write the poem in order to publicise this small masculine triumph, or because the whole encounter and its climax struck him as affecting and beautiful, or to punish one of the sisters or both? Inconceivable that it is only the first or the last of these; Archilochos is an odd mixture, but it would surely be wrong to dismiss him just as a selfish male tough, though he is that among other things.

It is here that the exegesis of scholarship can be valuably supplemented by the sympathetic vision of a fellow-artist. I for one have been enormously helped by Michael Ayrton's creative sympathy for Archilochos, and by the images he drew from it. The intensity of that sympathy, which is not devoid of a certain wariness, stands out from Michael Ayrton's own Introduction. It was his eccentricity, part of his creative and interpretative gift, to become possessed from time to time by other and earlier artists, or their myths: by Daedalus, by Berlioz. Near the end of his life it was Archilochos who became his daemon. For him, this ancient avatar was shaped by those islands and waters – stark and rugged like the Cycladic landscape, languid, moody or violent like the Aegean sea. His decision to draw the poet naked seems brilliantly right. It enabled him to escape from the misleading associations of vase-paintings, which for clothing and military equipment tend in any case to be either too sketchy or too fussy. More important, it enabled him to display the whole contradictory organism of his subject, complete with the obsessive facial features, the hard limbs and torso of a man of sea and hills, the belly and penis that controlled much of his life and poetry.

What else emerges from Michael Ayrton's drawings? Much more that is suggestive for anyone who struggles to understand his remarkable subject. The decomposed sprawl of Poseidon's sea-victims, curiously matching the languid flow of Archilochos' girls, almost Hellenistic in the artist's eyes in their speculative decadence. The beasts he has lifted out of context and presented as portraits, as self-contained symbols; all except for Myrmex, the ant who gives his name to a man, where the two-dimensional image offers a brilliant intuition of the force, as it might be, of those mysterious and incoherent verses. The savage fate Archilochos calls down on his enemy, the comrade who betrayed his oaths, on the seashore in Salmydessos, among the top-knotted Thracians. The terror of the elements, in storm or eclipse, which Ayrton isolates at the expense of the conventional trope to which Archilochos' poem, in frag. 122 (p. 18), devolves. The prickly pine-covered ridge of Thasos seen over the interlacing waves, with that sinister cloud clamped to its peak. And again the landscape of Paros itself, linear and tectonic, interlocking planes of rock softened in the foreground by the fig tree, symbol of femininity and ripeness.

That particular image depends largely on frag. 331 (p. 10), which compares a fig tree in the rocks, whose fruit only crows can reach, to a woman "loved by all". This is one of several fragments whose authenticity has been doubted. Michael Ayrton felt it to be all right, and I agree; the objections depend on taking *pasi philē*, "loved by all", as a proper name, which it may never have been. So too the Salmydessos fragment (p. 34), unascribed in its single papyrus source, has been judged by some scholars to belong to Archilochos, by others to Hipponax; I feel the former to be the more probable, and Michael agreed. Certain other fragments require the briefest of comments. Frag. 324 (p. 8) (*Tēnella kallinike*) is probably traditional in part, but was associated with Archilochos as early as Pindar's time. In frag. 19 (p. 6) the "craft" is not strictly in the Greek but alludes to Aristotle's information that Archilochos put these verses in the mouth of "Charon the carpenter". The second verse of frag. 205 (p. 22) is a reasonable supplement of the sense by the translator. The first two fragments on the same page, 172 and 173, come from the epode attacking Lykambes through the fable of the fox and the eagle, later incorporated in Aesop; fragments 174, 176 and 177 (pp. 24, 26) are from the same poem. Frag. 41 (p. 26) is probably an obscene reference to Neoboulé, and so is frag. 35 (p. 30).

Michael Ayrton did not wish to incorporate every one of the surviving fragments, although little of substance is omitted. This was never intended as a complete treatment on any level. At the same time it seems to me to offer more than fine editions usually do. His translations alone have a wit and compactness that bring out much of the feeling of the Greek; but it is the images facing them that project us into a quite unusual contact with one of the earliest, strangest and most powerful masters of lyric poetry.

A short bibliography

Text

West, M. L., *Iambi et Elegi Graeci*, vol. I (Oxford, O.U.P., 1971)
[The most reliable text, with full apparatus; does not include the Cologne epode, for which see:]

Page, D. L., *Supplementum Lyricum Graecum* (Oxford, O.U.P., 1974)

Text, translation and commentary

Lasserre, F., and Bonnard, A., *Archiloque* (Paris, Les Belles Lettres, 1958)
[Speculative, unreliable, sometimes interesting.]

Tarditi, G., *Archiloco* (Rome, Edizioni dell' Ateneo, 1968)

Treu, M., *Archilochos* (Munich, Heimeran, 1959)

There is no recent scholarly commentary in English, but a small selection of the poems, with helpful comments, is to be found in:

Campbell, D. A., *Greek Lyric Poetry, a Selection* (London, Macmillan, 1967)

General discussions

Fondation Hardt, *Entretiens*, vol. 10, *Archiloque* (Geneva-Vandoeuvres, 1963)
[Seven studies on technical aspects.]

Kirkwood, G. M., *Early Greek Monody* (Ithaca, N.Y., and London, Cornell U.P., 1974)
[The chapter on Archilochos is clear and useful.]

West, M. L., *Studies in Greek Elegy and Iambic* (Berlin, de Gruyter, 1974)
[Explains some points of detail arising out of his edition of the text; a scholar's aid, prohibitively expensive.]